I0016298

NOT JUST ANOTHER COMPUTER BOOK TWO FOR ADVANCED USERS

BY

ALFONSO J. KINGLOW PhD

Alfonso J. Kinglow

Copyright © 2016 Alfonso J. Kinglow

All rights reserved.

ISBN: **1508654786**
ISBN-13: **978-1508654780**

DEDICATION

This book is dedicated to my wife Sarah, for her kindness
and devotion, and for her endless support, and to my
grand-daughters
Karmelita, and Anaiah, and my grand-son Kenneth
who inspired it.

CONTENTS

Graphic Figures in Box Format

PREFACE

This book pick's up where *Not Just Another Computer Book,* the first one; left off. It is tailored for intermediate to advanced users and contains a lot more information and graphics that will clarify and explain in a more comprehensive format new technologies and techniques available today. The user is introduced to the new Wireless Standards 802.11 **ac** and **ad** and to Windows operating systems, networking, servers, tablets, cellphones and other mobile devices. You also learn about planning, designing and installing computers and Networks in many different ways, using different techniques.

Not Just Another Computer Book Two for Advanced Users, provides background and experience with many hidden built in utilities and experience with the latest computer technologies with WAN and LAN hardware and software. Computer and Networking Protocols are explained in detail in a more clear and comprehensive manner with clear examples. No prior computer experience is needed, although reading the first book and some experience in using a computer will be helpful. Basic experience with Windows 7 or 8 operating systems is also helpful.

This second book explains the Security Configuration and Analysis tool that is built in and hardly used, and the ability of the user to setup and configure the security of their own machines without using any external software or hardware.

It also introduces the user to the CMD Command Line Interpreter and the NET Commands that can be used to monitor and configure devices as well as manage the computer.

It also explores the different Anti Virus software, and explains the different Viruses affecting computers today, and how to eradicate them.

The Microsoft Management Console (MMC) that is built-in, is explained in detail, so the user can implement and manage many parts of the computer without using any external software.

Many hidden utilities are presented and revealed, some of which are built- in and others are visible in plain sight from the desktop, but not yet revealed to the user's.

This second book is intended for users that have some basic knowledge of computers and or can use a computer and navigate the Internet, but do not know the internal workings of a computer, the hidden Codes or all the hidden built-in Utilities and Configurations available to the user for free.

Information is presented to the user on many different available Software, Utilities and Applications that are free, and how to get them and install them on the computer.

Designing and implementing a *Dedicated Power System* for the computer is presented to the user, with the different types of batteries and their implementation. *Grounding* is explained in detail as a very important part of computers.

The Windows operating system is evolving rapidly and the users can expect a new Windows operating system, Code name **Windows 10** by the time of Publication of this book.

This book includes the following features:

1. The Chapters are in Spanish and English

2. Screen Captures, Illustrations and Graphics

3. Advanced Networking and Tools

4. Network Concepts and Configuration Techniques

5. Advanced Computer Terms

Additional information have been added to this book to help the user better understand what is been discussed in the Chapter. It may reference another Chapter in the book to clarify a point or present a new one., by including a Tip from the author's experience to provide extra information about how to configure and setup a computer, apply a concept, or solve a problem.

CHAPTER ONE

UNO

The Hardware

Any Computer will have the following three things: The Input, The Output and the ALU (Arithmetic Logic Unit). The Input is the keyboard and mouse and or any other device used to enter information into the computer. The output is the computer video display or monitor, and the ALU is the heart of the computer which contains the Processor, Memory and Storage.

In order to run the operating systems that we have today, the Computer hardware must meet a minimum requirement.

The Processor should be an Intel Processor, above 2.0 Ghz. Any Processor that is below 2.0 Ghz will be very slow. The most popular Intel Processors are 2.5 Ghz, or 2.8Ghz or higher, for faster speed, Intel have the Dual-Core Processors i-3, i5, i7 and higher.

The Installed RAM memory should be a minimum of 4 GB., where 8 GB is better. Computers with 3GB and 6 GB are not recommended; as portions of the RAM memory is been shared with the Display and does not follow the conventional memory division. Computer Memory is never odd numbers, but always follow the Standard of 1, 2, 4, 8,16, 32, and 64 GB etc...

Most computer display's will be 15 to 17 inch LCD (Liquid Crystal Display) if you are using a Lap Top, with a High Resolution of 1024 X 768 or higher. Much higher resolutions can be obtained with a Flat Screen Digital Monitor, that will also be an LCD or Plasma Display.

The Hard Drive or Internal Storage are usually 500 GB (Gigabytes) to 1 TB (Terabyte). The computer should not have a storage capacity of less than 500 GB., however; One Terabyte (1 TB) is preferred and recommended.

The Network Card also called a NIC (Network Interface Card or Network Adapter, should be a one Gigabyte Ethernet or Gigabit Ethernet as a minimum; and the Network Wireless Card should meet the new Standard for Wireless Networks 802.11/a/b/g/n/ **ac** or **ad.** The minimum Wireless Network Card should be 802.11/a/b/g/**n.**

Most computers will have 2 to 4 USB(Universal Serial Bus) Ports, The new standard for Computer Ports is USB 3.0 instead of the older 2.0 version.

The new version is downward compatible with the older USB 2.0 versions. Computers with the new USB 3.0 Ports will accept devices that still function with the older USB 2.0 Ports, using the USB 3.0 Cable with the older USB 2.0 Plug. Any and all devices that plug into your computer will do so through the USB Ports on the computer. Devices include Printers, Cameras, Keyboard, Mouse, Flash Drives and external storage devices, etc..

There is another very important Port that is now available on the newer computers, this Port is a Multimedia Port called, HDMI (High Definition Multimedia Interface) this Port is used to connect Multimedia devices from your computer to a Television to stream Audio and Video with many other uses. It requires an HDMI Cable with a Plug that is very similar to a USB Cable. The HDMI Port is also very similar to a USB Port.

Be very careful not to connect your USB Cable to an HDMI Port on your computer, you will damage the Port.

Most computers will have a built-in Web Cam or Camera. Some Web-cams are also external and connect to the computer via a USB Port. Most Web-Cams have built-in Microphones, so no external microphone is needed

CHAPTER TWO

DOS

The Software and Internet

The computer software are the programs that run the computer, the main Software program is the Application Software.

Many Applications are available for the Windows OS, some of these applications are: Printing Applications, Game Applications, Word Processing Applications, Office Applications, Multimedia Applications, Drawing and Painting Applications, and Network Applications.

Word Processing Applications are Microsoft Word, Notepad, Word Pad, etc.. Office Applications are contained in Microsoft Office Suite.

Multimedia Applications are Windows Media Player, CD/DVD Burner Applications, such as Nero and a few others.

Drawing and Painting Applications are Paint, Adobe Illustrator, Adobe Photoshop, Adobe Premier, etc.. Network Applications are Port

Scanner, Network Monitor, Net Surveyor, WiFi
, etc..

In Windows OS (Operating Systems) Windows
seven or eight and the new Windows 10 coming
out soon; Applications need to be Installed, so
that the user can Run them.

To remove an Application, it is necessary to use
a program called an UN-installer if the
Application was Installed. If the Application
was Setup by the user or by a Wizard, then it
can be Deleted.

Windows Applications have two kinds of
Installations; User Install and System Install.
The user must follow the installation
instructions to get the Software to run and
perform correctly. The System installation is
done by the Windows System, and does not
require User intervention.

Some Utilities written for Windows are treated
the same way as Applications for Installation or
Removal. Understanding the concept between
the two is very important.

The Application Software is divided into
Packaged Software, Custom Software, System
Software, Freeware, Public Domain, Shareware

or Trialware Software, and User Software.

The Application Software contains, Spreadsheet, Database, Graphics, Project Management, Medical Software, Scientific, Travel, Education Multimedia Entertainment and Multimedia Video and Audio.

The Packaged Software usually will contain Software Suite, a collection of multiple programs assembled into one package, such as Microsoft Office Suite, or Apache Open Office Suite, to name a few.

Freeware Software are programs and Utilities placed on the Internet for Free, that can be used and downloaded for free. Some of these Free software can be modified and re-packaged for distribution elsewhere.

Trialware also called Shareware are programs that are placed on the Internet for users to try and usually will have an expiration date of 15 to 30 days. Some of these programs are not complete and are only presented to the user as Demonstration of their product.

Public Domain Software is free and available on the Internet to download and use. These are complete and tested programs, and can be changed and modified, if needed. They are many different types of Software Programs in the Public Domain and available on the Internet for free use. One of these programs is Open Office from Apache.

Because Application Software is so important in Computers, Support Tools are sometimes needed and are provided in various formats and places to help the user.

Support Tools can be found in the following places: Online Help where you can find User Manuals, and can download them free. Web based Help from various Websites that contain FAQ (Frequently Asked Questions) and Chat Rooms., and Wizards, such as the Memo Wizard or the Help Wizard.

Most Application Software will contain Support Tools for Digital Video, Audio and Video Compression, and Windows Movie Maker. This Support Tool will allow the users to transfer video from a Camera, choose a Codex or Audio Format and choose a File format to Encode Audio and Video.

The File Formats are: .MOV and .QT an Apple Computers Quicktime Format, .WMV and .ASF a Microsoft Windows Media Format and .RM and RAM a RealNetworks Realmedia Format. All of these File formats are used to Encode Audio and Video.

Computer Technology today is found in the following areas: Industry, where computer standards are required and implemented in both the Digital and Analog World. In Academia, with many Multimedia Applications, Email and Video. In Scientific, Military and Government with the Internet and Arpanet, and with the Internet Protocols used in Networks Wan and Lan used by Computers.

Technology is used today in Computers Hardware and Software, Processors made by Intel and AMD, and hardware in Desktops and Laptops with Wireless Network Adapters. The Hardware and Software Technology also applies to Users and Business. The Technology in Windows also include Windows Security; with several software packages to include the following: Security Configuration and Analysis Tool, Windows Firewall, Windows Defender, MMC Microsoft Management Console with Snap-Ins and Windows Security with Secpol.exe Security Policy and Gpedit.exe Group Policy Editor. All of these Technologies are secured and are an integral part of Windows Security.

The Internet

The Internet is the largest WAN (Wide Area Network) in the World. The Internet was developed in 1960 and the World Wide Web (WWW.) in 1990. Internet service requires accessing the World Wide Web or (www.) which contains many Web sites. Each Web site will have a Web Address that identifies the Website location on the Internet.

Web sites contain many Web pages that displays the content of the Web site, usually the first page will be an Index html page that identifies the Web site. The World Wide Web is a collection of Electronic Documents called a Web Page. A Web Browser is an Application Software to access Web Pages.

The Internet uses Protocols to communicate and navigate the World Wide Web. It is important to understand what are these Protocols, and how to use them.

What are Protocols. Protocols are Standards, Rules and Regulations that tell the computer how to function and what to do to navigate the Internet. The first Protocol used is; http (Hyper text transport protocol) this protocol must be typed into a location on the Web Page called a URL (Universal Resource Locator) followed by a colon: and two slashes. (http://) the www. Is added with the name location of the Web page the user is trying to access. For example: (http://www.google.com) a Protocol Suite is used to establish the communication on the Internet Network. This Protocol is the Internet Protocol with the Transport Control Protocol, and its called; TCP/IP without this no communication on the Internet can be established.

TCP/IP is embedded in the Windows Network System to allow and facilitate communications over the Internet. In order to use the Internet, Windows Software requires an Application called a Web Browser. Microsoft Windows Web Browser is called IE or Internet Explorer. Web Pages are an Integral part of a Web Browser., and are written in a language called (html) Hypertext Markup Language, so that they can be displayed on the Internet. There are many different Web Browser's available for the Internet such as FireFox, Opera, Safari, Bing, and others.

Web Browser's contain many Web Pages that

can be viewed by the user. Some Web Browser's contain many Search Engines, to facilitate and help the users find what they are looking for on the Internet.

The Internet Protocol identifies computers on the Internet Network with a number. This number is called an IP address (198.85.147.35) the first three number groups identifies the network, and the last number identifies the computer. The Protocol www.google.com identifies the company and a Top Level Domain. There are many top level domains on the Internet., and are regulated by several Organizations. ICANN (Internet Corporation for Assigned Names and Numbers) also known as International Consortium of Assigned Names and Numbers, is one of several organizations regulating the Internet.

A DNS Server is a Computer that is running special software that stores and translates Domain Names into IP Addresses. Some Top Level Domains on the Internet are: .COM, .EDU, .INFO, .GOV, .MIL, .NET, .ORG,. To name a few.

On computers Internet Service is provided for E-Mail, FTP(File Transfer Protocol),

Newsgroups, Chat Rooms, IM Instant
Messaging, E-Mail addressing using
communications technology for POP Post
Office Protocol and SMTP Simple Mail
Transfer Protocol.. Because the Internet is the
largest Wide Area Network in the world, it uses
special WAN equipment and devices that are
different from the LAN Equipment, that you
would normally use in a small network or home
network.

The Internet uses an Internet Protocol (IP)
address number to identify the network, the
network class and the users machine on the
Internet WAN. A protocol suite called TCP/IP
or Transport Control Protocol/ Internet
Protocol is required in order to connect to the
Internet. The Internet uses both Public and
Private Addressing to communicate over the
Internet World Wide Web.

The TCP/IP number will usually be identified
by the numbers 192.168.30.5 or similar, where
the first numbers identify the network and
domain, and the last numbers the user's
machine.

Two types of IP addresses are used to identify
the user's computer on the Internet. A Static IP

Address is assigned to the user computer by an Administrator of the Network or a Dynamic IP Address is assigned automatically by a Domain Controller Server via DHCP Protocol. If a DHCP Domain Server is not available, and the user's computer don't have any IP address when it is first turned on, then a Private IP Address is assigned to it automatically by APIPA (Automatic Private IP Addressing) a built in Protocol in Windows OS.

CHAPTER THREE

TRES

Computer Communication

Computer Communication begins when Windows OS, versions seven, eight or ten starts. Windows will check Ram Memory to see if the Hardware is at least 2GB (Gigabytes), but 4 GB (Gigabytes) is preferred, The Processor speed is checked to see if its above 2.0 GHz or higher, or if the Processor is single core or Dual-core. If the single Processor is below 2.0 GHz, like 1.5 or 1.8 GHz; then the computer will be slow. If the computer Processor is a dual-core processor, then the computer will be very fast and will be determined by its "i " factor, such as " i-5, i-7, made by Intel.

Intel Dual Core Processors are very fast and are used in most computers.

Next the Hard Drive or Storage is checked to see if Storage is at least 500GB (Gigabytes) for Drive C:> but One Terabyte (1 TB) will be preferred. Next, a System Security Check is performed as part of the built-in Post or (Power-On-Self-Test) after Windows Modules are loaded, the following areas are checked: Control Panel, All Programs Installed, All System Programs, All Utilities (Built-In and User Installed) Network Cards or Adapters (Wired and Wireless) , Security and User Accounts.

The Desktop Display is presented to the User so that the User may Log-In and Start the User Programs.

 The Windows OS Processor plays an important role in the Post (Power-On-Self-Test) by checking the Storage Hard Drive C:> and Ram Memory Modules, the Keyboard and Mouse and the Start and Run Modules in Windows OS;

In the Control Panel programs that Run Windows are checked, Date and time is Set, Network and Protocols are Set, User Accounts, System Programs and Windows Utilities, Printers and other Devices and all Programs installed on the Computer.

A Word about Windows 10

Windows 10 is the most recent release of Windows. Because this is a new operating system it is not necessary to upgrade your machine immediately to this new OS. If you are using Windows 8 or 8.1 you should continue to use the OS and check first to see if your hardware can be upgraded to Windows 10.

Windows 10 requires a minimum hardware configuration to run which includes a Dual Core processor or higher that is at least above 2.0 GHz and a minimum Memory Ram of 4 GB but prefers 8 GB.

Because of future development, the hardware should have at least 1 Tb. (terabyte) For storage and the Wireless Network Card or Adapter should meet the new Wireless Standard 802.11**AC** or **AD.** The old wireless standard

802.11a/b/g/n will be too slow, and outdated.

Check the network adapters to make sure the hardware meets the minimum Requirements.

The fixed Ethernet Network Adapter Card inside the computer hardware, should be at least Gigabit Ethernet.

Some Basic info about Windows 10 users should know

Know how to sign out of Windows 10 Where's the option to sign out of Windows 10? Click your user account name at the upper-left of the Start Menu; a small panel will slide down from your name with "Sign out" listed. The fastest way to sign out remains as it was in prior Windows versions: Just press the Windows logo and "L" keys together, and you'll be instantly signed out.

Pick whatever accent color you want You can change the accent color of Windows 10, but you're given only a limited palette of 48 colors to choose from under the Personalization page of the Settings app. But the classic Control Panel that's still in Windows 10 gives you tools to create nearly any color you want for the accent. In the classic Control Panel, this color picker is nested under "Appearance and Personalization," "Personalization" and "Color and Appearance."

Change Edge's default search engine from Bing to another one Microsoft's new browser in Windows 10, Edge, also uses Bing as its search engine, but it's not obvious right away how to change it, should you prefer a different one. If you look up the option to change the default search engine under the browser's settings, the buttons are grayed out. The first thing you need to do is visit the search engine's site. While the site is open in a tab in Edge, you then go to the browser's settings: Click the "More actions" button that's to the upper-right of the browser, select "Settings," scroll down and select "View advanced settings," scroll down to "Search in the address bar with," click "Bing (www.bing.com)" and click "<Add new>". The search engine's domain and name will appear listed in a sidebar. Click it, and finally click "Add as default."

Delay automatic updates over Wi-Fi Under the Home version of Windows 10, updates to the OS by Microsoft are automatically pushed out and installed. With the Pro, Enterprise and Education versions, you can defer updates "for several months," according to Microsoft, but security updates are exempt.

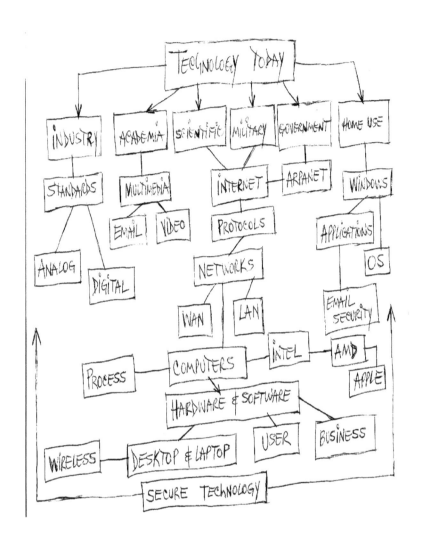

Technology Use Today

Figure 1.

Windows Application and System Software.

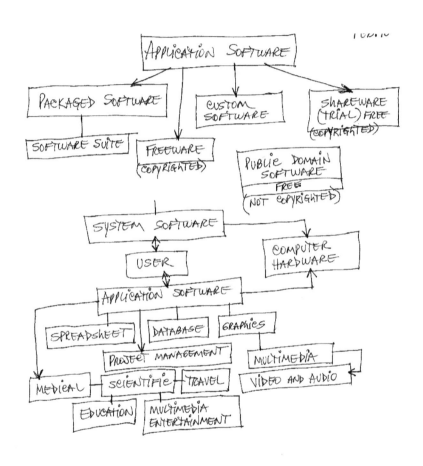

Figure 2.

Application Support and Tools.

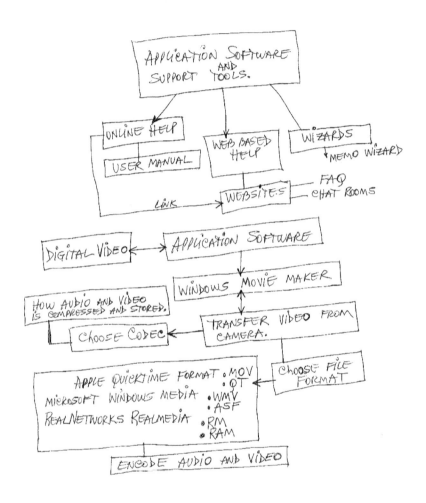

Figure 3.

Application Support and Tools

Type of Application Software.

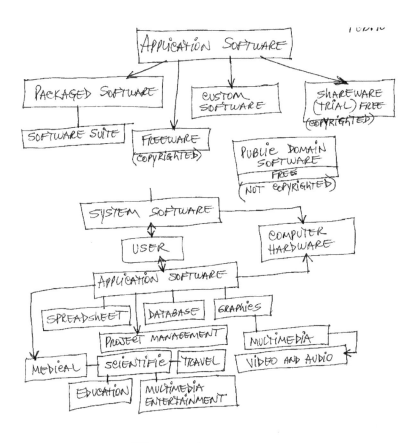

Figure 4.

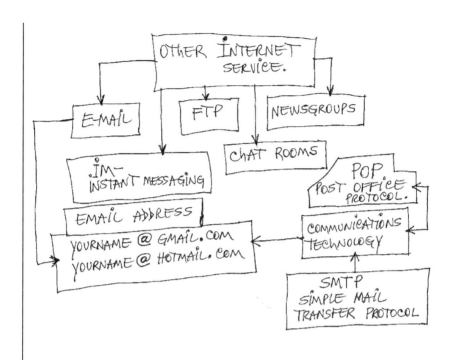

Other Internet Group Services

Figure 5.

MICROSOFT WORD KEY COMBINATION.——

COMMAND.	KEY COMBINATION	MENU COMMAND
COPY	SHIFT + F2 OR CTRL + C	EDIT	COPY
OPEN	CTRL + F12	FILE	OPEN
PASTE	CTRL + V	EDIT	PASTE

PRESS "NUM LOCK KEY"   LOCKS NUMERIC KEYPAD, SO YOU CAN...   USE KEYPAD TO TYPE NUMBERS.

DR. WATSON —— DIAGNOSTIC UTILITY —INCLUDED WITH XP.
MBSA (MICROSOFT BASELINE SECURITY ANALYZER)
(DOWNLOAD AND INSTALL)
FILE COMPRESSION UTILITY —— WINZIP AND PKZIP
COMPRESS (ZIP) AND UNCOMPRESS (UNZIP) FILES

THE COMMAND PROMPT TROUBLESHOOTING TASKS.——
"PING"   TEST TCP/IP CONNECTIVITY FOR INTERNET CONNECT.
"TRACERT"   TRACE DATA FROM YOUR PATH TO DESTINATION, EJ:
(TRACERT COURSE.COM)
"SYSTEMINFO"   FOR SYSTEM INFO.
"TASKLIST"   LIST OF PROCESSES RUNNING
"TASKKILL"   TERMINATE ANY PROCESS
(TASKKILL /PID 5168)
"CHKDSK"   CHECK DISK
"DEFRAG C:"   DEFRAGMENT DISK

Word Key Combination

Figure 6a.

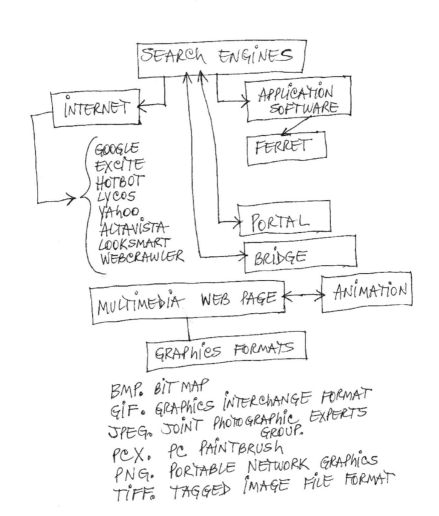

SEARCH ENGINES

INTERNET

GOOGLE
EXCITE
HOTBOT
LYCOS
YAHOO
ALTAVISTA
LOOKSMART
WEBCRAWLER

APPLICATION SOFTWARE

FERRET

PORTAL

BRIDGE

MULTIMEDIA WEB PAGE ← → ANIMATION

GRAPHICS FORMATS

BMP. BITMAP
GIF. GRAPHICS INTERCHANGE FORMAT
JPEG. JOINT PHOTOGRAPHIC EXPERTS GROUP.
PCX. PC PAINTBRUSH
PNG. PORTABLE NETWORK GRAPHICS
TIFF. TAGGED IMAGE FILE FORMAT

Search Engines.

Figure 6b.

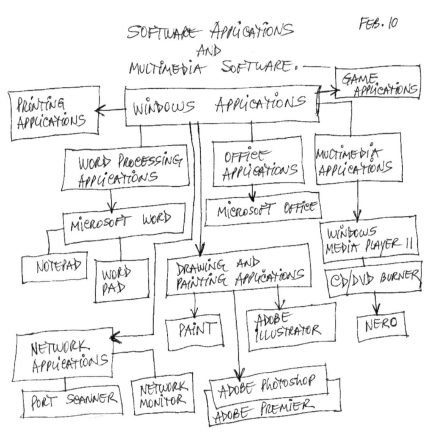

SOFTWARE APPLICATIONS
AND
MULTIMEDIA SOFTWARE.

FEB. 10

NOTE:

INSTALL APPLICATIONS VS. RUN APPLICATIONS
UNINSTALL APPLICATIONS VS. DELETE APPLICATIONS
ADD AND REMOVE APPLICATIONS (SOFTWARE)
UTILITY VS. APPLICATIONS
USER INSTALL VS. SYSTEM INSTALL APPLICATIONS

Windows Applications

Figure 6c.

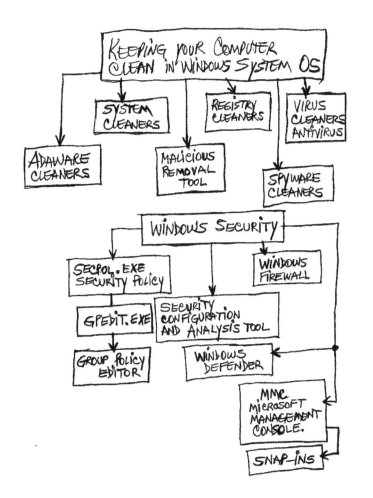

Keeping your Computer Clean.

Keeping your Computer Clean Information

One of the most important things to know about how to keep your computer hardware and software clean and free of viruses, is to understand the different parts of the computer that needs to be cleaned.

The most important part is the Registry, the heart of Windows OS, it requires a special kind of cleaner designed only for the Registry, mentioned in this book; such as ADVANCED SYSTEM CARE 9 and ACEBYTE UTILITIES 3.0, the other part is the System, which deals with the performance of the hardware, and requires cleaners designed for that area, such as CLEAN MASTER and GLARY UTILITIES 5.42

The other part of the Computer that protects the hardware and software are the Antivirus programs and Malicious Removal Tools, a Utility from Microsoft that takes care of Spywares and Malware, mentioned in this book.

Many Antivirus programs are available on the Internet, and the user have the choice to get the FREE versions or the PAID versions, they all do a good job. We recommend using the FREE version first, and recommend the .AVG Antivirus new 2016 ZEN which is free.

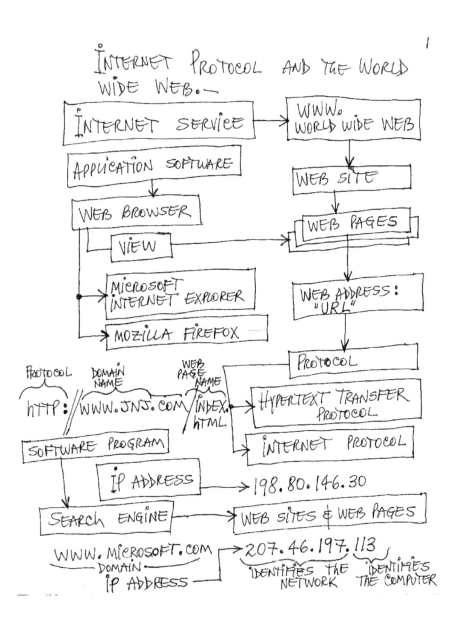

Figure 7.

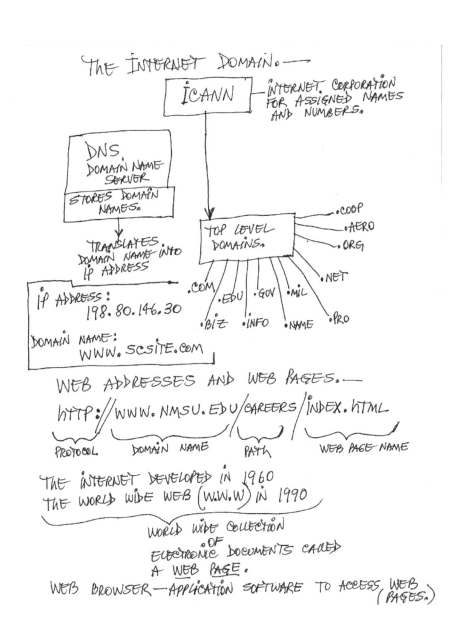

THE INTERNET DOMAIN. ——

ICANN — INTERNET. CORPORATION FOR ASSIGNED NAMES AND NUMBERS.

DNS. DOMAIN NAME SERVER
STORES DOMAIN NAMES.

TRANSLATES DOMAIN NAME INTO IP ADDRESS

TOP LEVEL DOMAINS.

.COOP
.AERO
.ORG
.NET

.COM .EDU .GOV .MIL
.BIZ .INFO .NAME .PRO

IP ADDRESS: 198.80.146.30
DOMAIN NAME: WWW.SCSITE.COM

WEB ADDRESSES AND WEB PAGES. ——

http://www.nmsu.edu/careers/index.html

PROTOCOL   DOMAIN NAME   PATH   WEB PAGE NAME

THE INTERNET DEVELOPED IN 1960
THE WORLD WIDE WEB (W.W.W) IN 1990

WORLD WIDE COLLECTION OF ELECTRONIC DOCUMENTS CALLED A WEB PAGE.

WEB BROWSER — APPLICATION SOFTWARE TO ACCESS WEB (PAGES.)

Figure 8.

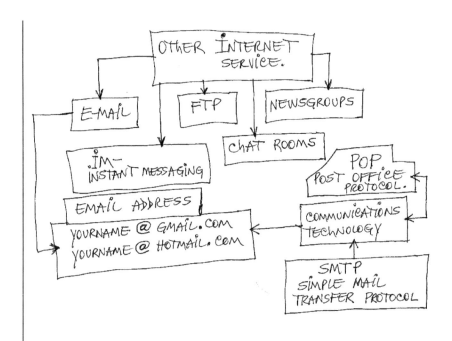

Other Internet Service.

Figure 9.

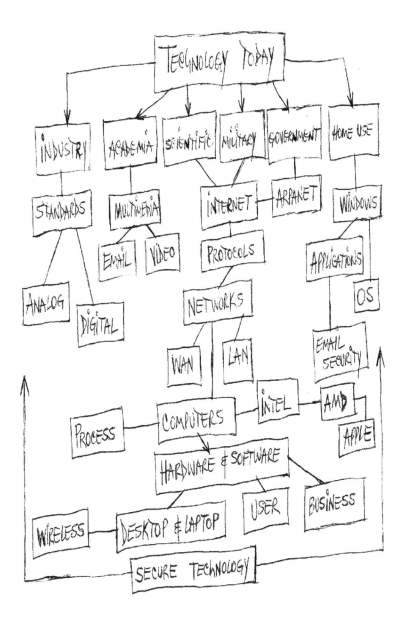

Technology Today Expanded

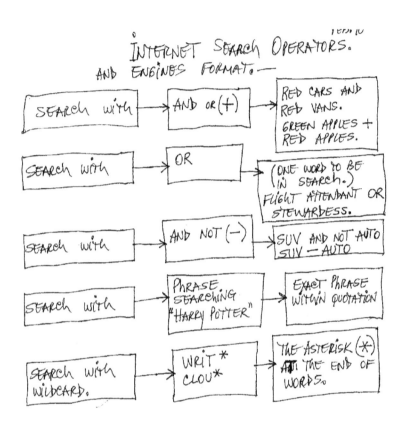

Search Operators on the Internet

Figure 10.

CHAPTER FOUR

CUATRO

Computer Cables and Wires in Networking

Networking

Computers that are connected together with printers, other computers, network equipment, linked by radio or cables or a wireless medium, sharing information, documents, data, video, voice, media and other resources is called a Network. They are many different types of Networks, the most common are LAN's (Local Area Networks) and WAN (Wide Area Networks) used for long distance communication between networks. The Internet is the largest WAN in the World.

Other Networks are PAN (Personal Area Networks) and CAN (Campus Area Network) owned by a University and MAN Metropolitan Area Networks, in large cities.

Networks that connect many different types of users with different equipments and other networks, are called " Enterprise Networks" and are used in large organizations.

LAN Local Area Networks are used in offices and homes where a few computers are connected to share resources and data or in a computer Lab where several computers are connected to exchange information and share resources.

WAN Networks are used for long distance communication between cities and or countries, and usually require a Satellite link and special equipment.

Network Properties

There are four Network Properties used to distinguish one type of Network from another.

- Communications medium used, Air, Cable, Fiber, or Satellite.

- Protocol

- Topology

- Network type, Private or Public

A private network is owned by an Organization such as a CAN (Campus Area Network) A public network offer services to the public such as Verizon, ATT, or a Cable Network TV Company.

Topology

Topology is the Physical layout of a Network with combination of cabling, equipment, workstations and software. The most popular and used topology is the Star, and Bus, The Mesh, Tree and Ring topologies are used to provide redundancy, failsafe and high data rate access.

The Bus Topology connects a cable from one computer to the next, and a terminator at each end and must meet IEEE (Institute of Electrical and Electronics Engineers) Standard for this type of network.

A Ring topology is a continuous data network with no logical beginning or ending point with no terminations, and is used for high data rate using Optical Networks, which require using FiberOptics Cable.

A Star topology is the most popular and oldest design method, it uses a central device called a Hub or Switch, that join single cable network segments or individual LAN's into one network.

A Mesh topology connects every other segment to every other one, to provide Fault Tolerance and Redundancy in case of equipment failure.

Two types of Services are used for communications in a network. Connectionless Service and Connection-Oriented service. In a connectionless service Frames are not checked if they are received ok and there is no error recovery.

In a connection-oriented service , the frame-sequence number is checked, the receiving side sends an ACK or acknowledgement that the data was transmitted successfully, and error's are detected.

A Packet is a discrete data unit formatted as a Signal for transmission over a network.

A Frame is a discrete data unit transmitted that contains control and address information, but no Routing Information.

Analog Signal

 Network Signals are Analog or Digital. Analog signal vary continuously in the form of a wave with Positive and Negative voltage levels. A radio or telephone signal is an analog transmission. Analog transmission is used in WAN's that use analog modems for communication over a telephone line.

Digital Signal

A digital signal uses exact voltage level to generate zero's and one's or binary numbers, it's the most common signaling method used on LAN

 And high speed WAN's. A +5 volts can produce a one, and a 0 zero volts can produce a zero.

All networks used a Standard called " The OSI Reference

Model ", or Open Systems Interconnect.

The OSI Networking Model was developed by several International organizations; ISO (International Standard Organization) , ANSI (American National Standards Institute) and ITU (International Telecommunication Union); these organizations developed the Network Protocol Standards in 1970.

The OSI Model applies to all LAN and WAN communications and standardize network software and hardware. The OSI Model consist of 7 Layers stack on one another, and are: The Physical Layer, Data Link, Network, Transport, Session, Presentation and Application, each layer handles specific communications tasks. And use specific Protocols.. The Physical Layer is Layer 1. The Data Link is Layer 2. The Network layer is Layer 3. The Transport Layer is Layer 4. The Session Layer is Layer 5. The Presentation is Layer 6. and the Application Layer is Layer 7. And its on the Top of the Stack. The Physical Layer is at the bottom.

The Data Link Layer organizes Bits (0/1) and Formats them into Frames.

The Network Layer controls the passage of Packets on routes on the Network, and routes them along the most efficient paths.

The Transport layer identifies the value assigned to each circuit or Port, a connection identification; or a Socket which is assigned by the Session Layer.

The Session Layer establishes and maintain the communications link between two nodes, and determines how long they can transmit. When you use your Computer to communicate over the Internet, your workstation use a unique Internet Protocol (IP) address number. The Session Layer uses this number to establish contact between nodes.

The Internet protocol used on your Computer is IPv4 and IPv6 which is the latest version.

The Presentation Layer manages Formatting, because Software Applications use different Data Formats. The Presentation Layer is also responsible for Data Encryption, a process that scrambles the data to secure it from intruders.

The Application Layer is the highest Level of the OSI Model. This Layer is used by Computer programmers to connect workstations to Network Services.. This Layer gives computer user's direct access to Applications and network Services. Microsoft Windows Redirector works through the Application Layer.

The PING utility is used to Test network adapters and

connections by using the Address: 127.0.0.1 a loopback address which is the address used for a testing network cards .

LAN Transmission Methodology

Two main LAN Transmission methods are used for Networks: Ethernet (IEEE 802.3) standard, and Token Ring (IEEE 802.5) standard.

Ethernet is a LAN Standard that uses the Star and Bus Topologies, with transmission rates from 100 Mbps, 1 Gbps, 10Gbps, 40 Gbps, and 100 Gbps.

Ethernet uses a control method called (CSMA/CD) Carrier Sense Multiple Access with Collision Detection. An Algorithm (Computer Logic) that transmits and Decodes formatted data Frames.

Ethernet only allows one node to transmit at a time. Transmission is done by sending a carrier signal. Sometimes more than one node transmits at the same time and this result in a collision. There is a collision detection software that allows the computer to recover from the collisions.

An Ethernet Frames contains the Preamble, Start of Frame, Destination address, the length, Data and Frame Check sequence.

WAN Network Communications

Wide Area Networks are used by telecom, cable TV and satellite companies. Their topologies and transmission techniques are very complex and are always changing.

The most basic WAN communication is done over public switched telephone networks and use over telephone lines with both analog and digital modems high speed access using DSL Digital Subscriber Line and ISDN Integrated Services Digital Network technologies.

They use dedicated telephone lines called T-carrier Line. The smallest T-carrier service is aprox. 1.4 Mbps and the largest is aprox. 500 Mbps called a T-5 Line and can contain over 300 switched channels.

Cable TV WAN uses Trunk Lines, a high capacity line between two switches that are over several miles away to provide service.

Wireless WAN use Radio, Microwave and Satellite communication antennas to transmit Radio wave to an Antenna that is far away that is connected to equipment to communicate using a method called Packet Radio at very high radio frequencies.

Cell phone providers offer several wireless transmission services, which are 2G Wireless, 3G Wireless, and 4G Wireless networks.

WAN Transmission Methodology

WAN Transmission methods use different switching techniques to create channels for high speed and to be efficient. The most used methods are:

1. Time Division Multiplex (TDM) access

2. Frequency Division Multiplex (FDM) access

3. Packet switching

4. Message switching

There are many options for connecting Ethernet networks to all types of WAN technologies.

They are standards for Cable Ethernet and Wireless Communications that are compatible with Ethernet and more forms of WAN switching Techniques.

CHAPTER FIVE

CINCO

Computer Devices and more

There are equipment devices used to connect to a simple network called a LAN Local Area Network. These devices can connect just a few computers or many computers in a large network. Some of these devices are:

- Repeaters (Class I and Class II)

- Hubs (Active and Passive)

- Bridges

- Routers

- Switches

- Brouters

- Gateways

Repeaters connect two or more segments on a network and can retransmit incoming signals. It can filter out noise caused by EMI/RFI. It can also amplify incoming signals and reshape it for better transmission. Repeaters are used to extend a cable segment or a wireless signal and can sense network problems and shut down the bad segment.

Switches are like bridges, but they can increase the bandwidth on networks. Switches can use the Spanning Tree

Algorithm to manage network traffic. Switches use two types of switching techniques called Cut Through Switching and Store and Forward Switching, which is the most popular, where the frame is not forwarded until its completely received. Switches can be Managed or Unmanaged.

Gateway is a Software or Hardware Box that permits two different types of networks to communicate. A gateway can translate different types of addresses, direct E-Mail to the right destination and connect networks with different architectures, like a TCP/IP Network to an IBM Network or an Apple Computer Network.

A Hub is a device or box that connects workstations and servers in a star topology. And can have many inputs and outputs active at the same time. A Hub is used to connect many computers from a central location and can connect many different types of computers having different connectors. It allows for centralized management of the network.

A Bridge only look at MAC addresses and can have up to 52 Ports, it is then called a

Multiport Bridge. Wireless Bridges are called Access Points. A bridge is used to connect one LAN to another LAN. Can segment a LAN to reduce traffic and prevent access to a LAN. The Bridge was replaced by the Router.

Routers direct data to specific computers. They have built in intelligence and are design for learning, filtering and forwarding. Routers are used to join distant networks and or networks that are close, they can connect dissimilar networks. Routers use a system called metric to determine the best route going through a network. They use static and dynamic routing. Dynamic routing is automatic. Routers work with a protocol called RIP. (Routing Information Protocol) which is limited to aprox. 15 Hops. The regeneration, amplification and movement of a data packet through the network is called a Hop. The most popular routing used by Routers is OSPF (Open Shortest Path First) where only a portion of the routing table is sent.

A network that have two or more bridges use the Spanning Tree Algorithm (STA) to setup a system of checks, to forward frames through the most efficient route and to make sure bridges don't get into an endless loop. Bridges communicate with one another using BPDU's (Bridge Protocol Data Units)

WAN Transmission Devices

This equipment is designed to work over Public Switched telephone networks using telephone lines like the T-carrier lines called T1 and the ISDN Lines called Integrated Services Digital Network, a standard for digital data services over telephone lines.

The most common WAN Devices that are used are:

- Analog telephone modems

- ISDN Adapters

- Cable TV Modems

- DSL Modems and Routers

- Servers

- Remote Router

Wireless Computers and Standards

The most popular Wireless networking technologies are:

1. Radio Wave Technologies, with Cellular

2. Infrared Technologies

3. Satellite and Microwave Technologies

The Standard that regulates Wireless Communications is IEEE project 802.11 a/b/g/n, **ac** or **ad.**

The new Wireless Standard is 802.11 a/b/g/**ac** or **ad.**

Advantages of Wireless Networks:

They are designed to accommodate all kinds of requirements; To provide communications where it would be difficult to install a wired network, Reduce Cost, provide easy Networking to a home or office, and provide access anywhere, not limited to a location.

The wireless components are: a Wireless network Adapter Card, an Access Point, a Directional Antenna, Omnidirectional antenna,

The Wireless Access Method used is CSMA/CA or Carrier Sense Multiple Access with Collision Avoidance.

Transmission Speeds are from 1 Mbps to 54 Mbps using Frequency of aprox. 2 to 5 GHz and from 1 GB (Gigabyte) up to 10 GB with the new Standards AC and AD and operating at Frequencies within the 5 GHz and higher.

The Security Techniques used for Wireless are a Shared Key Authentication or Wired Equivalent Privacy Key with 128 Bit Encryption. Also used is a Wi-Fi Protected Access Encryption Key Combination up to 256 Bit Key.

WPA2 is the newest version of WPA providing a stronger encryption method using AES Advanced Encryption Standard.

The 802.11 Wireless use two Topologies called

Independent Basic Service Set (IBSS)
Topology and The Extended Service Set (ESS)
Topology. This Topology use a much larger
service area that can extend the range of
Wireless Communications, and is used in large
Networks.

Alternative Radio Wave Technologies are
Bluetooth and HiperLan, which is used in
Europe. Bluetooth range can be extended
depending on the Class and Mode selected.
From a few feet to about 200 feet or more.

Cellular Phone Communications.

Cellular phones work with Packet Radio using
2G,3G and 4G Networks as a radio Transmitter
and Receiver. The range can be a few city blocks
or up to aprox. 300 miles depending on the
technology.

CHAPTER SIX

SEIS

Sharing Resources on your Computer

Peer to Peer Networking is used to configure a network and to share Resources and is used only for about 10 workstations.

There is no central management software to manage computers. This type of network only have basic moderate security and the user account must be managed by each workstation.

The peer to Peer network is slow and is not optimized for many users. It is normally setup for Home use. All computers can be seen by all other computers through the network discovery to manage shared resources such as Printers and other computers.

Network discovery is a Windows tool that manages how computers are seen on a network using three types of discovery: a) OFF where a computer can not view other computers on the network. b) ON where a Computer in a Home Group or Workgroup can view other computers on the Network. c) CUSTOM where the network Administrator configures specific network discovery rules, blocking discovery of certain computers.

CHAPTER SEVEN

SIETE

Applications and Utilities

They are Free and Paid Applications and Utilities on the Internet that can be downloaded for free to manage your Computer, and provide Security and all the necessary software to make the computer user more productive. Some of the Free Applications are: Word Processors like WordLib, and Open Office, that can be downloaded from open office.org and other Applications like Antivirus programs like the Free AVG Antivirus from avg.com and others.

They are many Free Utilities to keep your computer Registry clean and your computer Tuned up for better Performance. The most popular are: Advanced System Care 8.4, Glary Utilities version 5.36, Acebyte Utilities 3.2, Clean Master, Malaware Malabytes, etc..

All of these programs are free. The user can Google all or any of the programs or Utilities to go to the download webpage of the program.

These programs are designed to operate with Windows 7, 8.0 and 8.1 most programs will work with Windows 10 until new versions become available.

CHAPTER EIGHT

OCHO

Networks and the Internet

Networks connect computers and devices to share resources, such as information, hardware, software and data. A single printer which is a resource is shared via a network to multiple computers connected to a LAN local Area Network or a Wide Area Network WAN which is the largest Network in the world.

The main Internet service is the WWW or World Wide Web. This Internet service serves over 1 (One) Billion users(As of 2013) and is a world wide collection of networks that links individuals with resources and data.

The web contains Billions of Documents called Web Pages, and connects via an ISP Internet Service Provider or via an OSP Online Service Provider.

A Web page may contain text, graphics, sound and video and links to other Web documents. A

Web Site, such as Google, is a collection of related Web pages that require the use of a Web Browser, a Web application in order to view the web pages. An example of these Web Applications are: IE Internet Explorer, Mozilla Firefox, Safari, Opera etc..

These Applications display content, financial data, news, guides, weather, legal info and other.. The Future of the Internet is Internet 2, a New Technology that will contain new Standards by W3C World Wide Web Consortium, coming soon.

The Most Popular Search Engines on the Internet

The most important search engines on the Internet are the ones that use Semantic Searches and not Boolean Searches, which are the most popular. A very important Semantic Search Portal is " HAKIA" http://www.hakia.com

Semantics is the study of the meaning of a linguistic expression. The language can be a Natural Language, such as English or Navajo or an Artificial Language. It also deals with varieties and changes in the meaning of words, phrases, sentences and text.

The most Popular search engines are:

1. Google

2. Bing

3. Yahoo

4. Ask

5. Aol

6. Wow

7. WebCrawler

8. MyWebSearch

9. Infospace

10. eBizMBA

11. DuckDuckGo

12. Blekko

13. Contenko

14. Dogpile

15. Alhea

THE COMPUTER DESKTOP.

Main System Programs (System Control

Programs.)

1. My Computer
   My Documents
2. My Network Places
   My Recent Documents
3. Internet Explorer 8
   My Pictures
4. Antivirus Program (free AVAST or AVG)
   My Music
5. Adobe ACROBAT Reader
   My Computer

< START >   User Programs

<u>ALL PROGRAMS</u> > Accessories

Control Panel

                 Games

Set Program Access & Defaults

                 Startup

Printers and Faxes

                 Accessibility

                 Communications

Help and Support

                 Entertainment

Search

                 System Tools

Run

                 Command prompt C:>

                 NotePad

                 WordPad

USER CONTROLS..

1. Accessibility ---→ Accessibility Wizard
5. **System Tools (Continues)**

Magnifier

Schedule Tasks

Narrator

System Information

On Screen Keyboard

System Restore

Utility Manager

2. Communications ---→ HyperTerminal

Call another Computer

Network Connections

Network Setup Wizard

New Connection

Wireless Network Setup

Wizard

3. Entertainment------→ Sound Recorder
                        Volume Control

                    Windows Media Player 12

UTILITIES.

4. System Tools-----→ Backup – Disk Cleanup
   – Disk Defragmenter
                    File Settings Transfer –
Internet Explorer (No add-on's)

Blank.

CHAPTER NINE

NUEVE

The Special Advanced and Applications folder from hidden codes

This Procedure will create a special folder containing advanced files for troubleshooting and maintaining your computer in any situation.

The advanced folder will have over 200 files and applications to aid and show the user how to fix any problem(s) on the computer.

It is created from hidden codes built into the system. Follow the instructions exactly to create the folder.

To Create the Special Advance Folder:

CREATE A NEW FOLDER, CALL IT: ADVANCED.

Put a Period. After the D.

ENTER THE CODE AFTER YOU OPEN BRACKET, CLOSE BRACKET AT THE END.

OPEN BRACKET{

CLOSE BRACKET }

Advanced.{ED7BA470-8E54-465E-825C-99712043E01C}

And press <ENTER>

The new folder will be created, and will be different from any folder you have on your desktop.

Creating the All Applications Folder

The All Applications Folder allows the user to create a folder that will contain and consolidate all of the user Applications in one place and into one folder, which will save time and space as the user will not need to go to the Start and then Open all programs and then select the program to work on, as all the user applications and programs will be in one moveable and portable folder.

The user will then just open that folder to have access to all the applications at once and can   launch them directly from that location without Windows having to load the program every time the user wants to use it.

TO CREATE THE "ALL APPLICATIONS FOLDER"

Create a blank folder and label it: All Applications.   (period) is important.

Enter the Code:

All Applications.{4234d49b-0245-4df3-b780-3893943456e1}
press <enter> to create your "All Applications Folder".

Your folder will be created on the desktop, Open the Folder to display all of the applications.

A Word about Viruses

The first thing is to recognize that any program that is written to damage or harm your computer in any way should be considered as a Virus.

Also it is important to identify most viruses as a " Program" or Software, which means that some one wrote it, and that it can be deleted, modified,. erased, changed and quarentined. The Virus itself is vulnerable.

The greatest enemy of the Virus is another Software program, called the " Anti-Virus ". To protect all computers from Viruses, you will need an " ANTIVIRUS" program.

There are many Antivirus programs available. You can get FREE Antivirus programs and PAID Antivirus programs.

A very popular Free Antivirus program is the " Free AVG ANTIVIRUS 2016 " that can be downloaded from the Internet. The Free AVG Antivirus program will protect your computer with the BASIC protection it offers in 3 of its 6 or 7 categories.

The BASIC protection is all Home Users should need, however you may purchase a PAID Antivirus program to get the added capabilities if you have a business or many devices to protect.

DEFINITION OF VIRUSES ON THE INTERNET

A VIRUS is a Program that Spreads by Replicating itself into other programs or Documents.

A WORM is a self replicating program like a Virus, but does not Attach itself. It is a Self-Contained program.

A TROJAN is a Program that appears to be useful, but contains Malware. For example, a Utility Program.

A MALWARE is any Software Program designed to cause   harm.

A HOAX VIRUS is the worse kind of Virus, it sends hoax messages to users, and infects your E-Mail and Contacts on a computer.

A ROOT KIT is very dangerous form of a TROJAN, it Monitors traffic to and from your computer, and alters your System files; slowing down your computer.

A SPYWARE affects E-Mail, and monitors and Control part of your Computer, by decreasing your computer performance.

A SPAM is a nuisance, it is not a Threat, and is Unsolicited Mail.

ADAWARE is like A SPYWARE, it affects computer Performance.

They are many organizations on the Internet that would like you to report all or any Virus that you encounter on the Internet.

A Virus Database is maintained and kept up to date by AVG, Panda, and many other Antivirus Companies. As you install your Antivirus software, at the end the software will UPDATE automatically its VDF File or Virus-Definition-Files; this is very important as the software requires it before you can use the Antivirus program, in order to be up to date with the latest Viruses out on the internet and be able to offer the necessary protection against these viruses and any other new virus that may show up.

NOTE on VIRUSES:

A WORD ON PLUG-INS

What are Plug-Ins. These are small programs and or utilities that extend the capability of your Browser.

By installing a Plug-In into any of your Browsers (You may use more that one) for Example; IE Internet Explorer, Mozilla Firebox, Safari, Opera etc.. the user will enhance the Browser to be able to display Multimedia Elements embedded on a Web page on the Internet or to be able to display Real Time Multimedia Content on the Internet.

The following are FREE Plug-Ins available on the Internet.

FREE PLUG-INS AVAILABLE ON THE INTERNET

The following are FREE Plug-In Applications: For Graphic Animation FLASHPLAYER from macromedia.com; for MP3 and Audio CD LIQUID PLAYER from liquidaudio.com; for Live Audio and Video, REALONE PLAYER from real.com; for HD Music and HD video, QUICKTIME from apple.com, for Multimedia 3D Graphics, SHOCKWAVE PLAYER from macromedia.com, for .PDF Files ACROBAT READER, from adobe.com; from Microsoft Windows, WINDOWS MEDIA PLAYER.

Any one of these plug-Ins can be downloaded from the Internet and installed at any time into your computer browsers.

NOTES on MULTIMEDIA PLUG-INS.

CHAPTER TEN

DIEZ

Figures that applies to this book that is explained in

Graphic format.

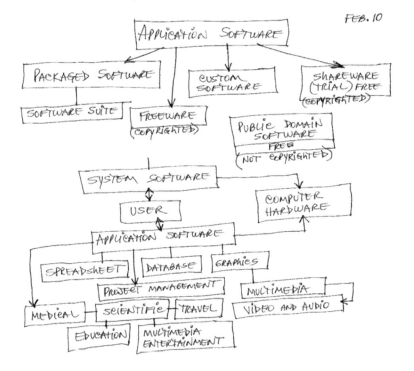

Application Software explained in graphic format.

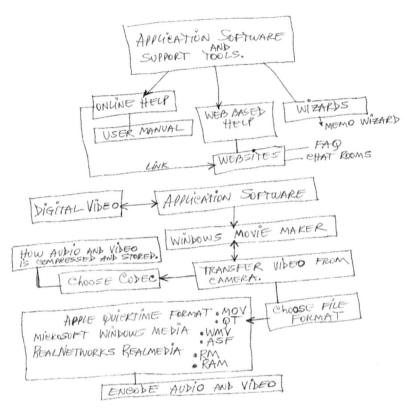

Application Software and Support Tools.

THE INTERNET DOMAIN. →

ICANN — INTERNET. CORPORATION
FOR ASSIGNED NAMES
AND NUMBERS.

DNS.
DOMAIN NAME
SERVER
STORES DOMAIN
NAMES.

TOP LEVEL
DOMAINS.

• COOP
• AERO
• ORG

• NET

TRANSLATES
DOMAIN NAME INTO
IP ADDRESS

.COM
.EDU   .GOV   .MIL
.BIZ   .INFO   .NAME   .PRO

IP ADDRESS:
198. 80. 146. 30

DOMAIN NAME:
WWW. SCSITE.COM

WEB ADDRESSES AND WEB PAGES. —

http://WWW.NMSU.EDU/CAREERS/INDEX.HTML

PROTOCOL   DOMAIN NAME   PATH   WEB PAGE NAME

THE INTERNET DEVELOPED IN 1960
THE WORLD WIDE WEB (W.W.W) IN 1990

WORLD WIDE COLLECTION
OF
ELECTRONIC DOCUMENTS CALLED
A WEB PAGE.
WEB BROWSER — APPLICATION SOFTWARE TO ACCESS WEB
(PAGES.)

The Internet Domain and examples.

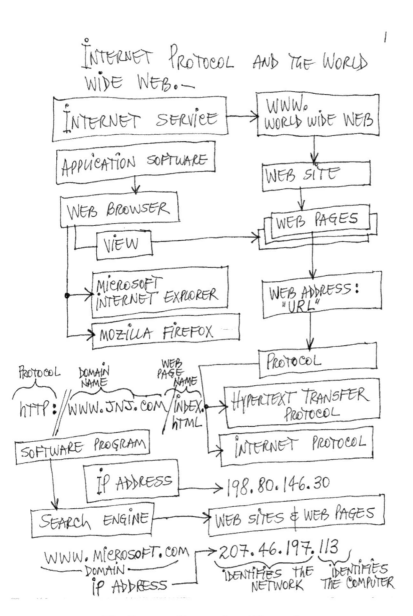

The Internet Protocol and Examples.

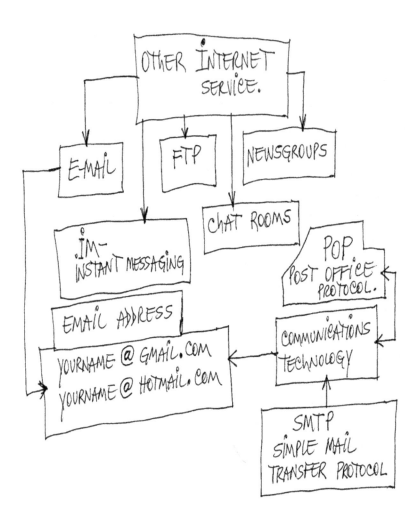

Other Internet Services.

Keeping your Computers Clean.

The graphics and text presented in the Book are Graphic Representation of Text in Block format for easy understanding of the Computer hardware and software processes.

Almost all of the Graphics were designed by hand using free drawing techniques with No.2 pencil.

The Graphic drawing " Keeping Computers Clean" displays the Free Utilities and Software available to everyone on the Internet, if you know where to look. I wanted to display this information so that everyone could go and have access to all the free software that is available to users and are not published anywhere.

There are Four (4) Types of Free Software you should look for on the Internet.

1. Applications   3. Antivirus

2. Productivity   4. Utilities

The User can find these Free software on the Internet in :
Public Domain, Open Source, Freeware and Trialware sections of the Internet.

Every Computer must be cleaned or maintained in three areas:
The System, The Registry and the Hardware Performance.

Network Monitoring Tools and Performance Monitor software

is built into every Windows OS.

The following Software Applications and Utilities are required to keep your Computer clean protected and up to date:

- ADVANCED SYSTEM CARE 9

- GLARY UTILITIES 5.40

- ACEBYTE UTILITY 3.0.2

- CLEAN MASTER 12.1

- MALABYTES ANTI-MALWARE 2.0 OR HIGHER

- SMART DEFRAG 4.0

- FREE .AVG ANTIVIRUS FREE BASIC EDITION 2016 ZEN PROTECTION.

All of these Software Applications and Utilities are Free and can be downloaded from the Internet at the locations I mentioned.

CHAPTER ELEVEN

ONCE

Computer Security and Troubleshooting

Computer Security is built into Windows and the User just need to activate it. Basic computer security is provided in the Control Panel with the Windows Firewall, which must be enabled.

Security can also be setup using the Security templates built into the MMC Microsoft Management Console.

Security in Windows is also setup by typing into the RUN or Start window, the Security Commands: SECPOL   which is the security policy, and also GPEDIT which is the Group Policy Editor.

Look at the Graphic Drawing" Keeping your Computer Clean in Windows System OS." Which applies to all and any Windows OS.

Local Security Setup using SECPOL in Windows.

If the command SECPOL does not work from the RUN window in Windows, the User can also launch it from the command Line **CMD,** by just typing CMD in the Run or Start location in Windows.

The same will work with GPEDIT the group policy Editor below.

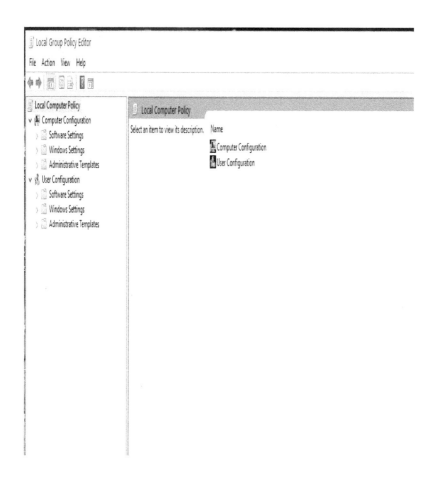

Group Policy Editor Setup in Windows.

NOTES.

CHAPTER TWELVE

DOCE

Basic Computer Terms, Acronyms and the Microsoft Management Console (MMC).

1. APPLICATION: another word for a program or software.

2. **BOLD:** A font style that makes letters and words darker.

These words are bold.

These words are not.

3. **CENTRAL PROCESSING UNIT:** where all of the information you put into the computer is stored.

4. **CLICKING**: Pointing to something on the screen

and then pushing the button
on the mouse is called
clicking.

5. **CURSOR**: The line or
arrow that follows your
mouse movement.

6. DESKTOP: The screen
you see first when your
computer turns on.

7. **DIALOGUE BOX**: A
window that pops up and
asks you questions.

8. **DISK DRIVE**: The place
where you put your disk so
that you can save files on it.

9. DISKS: Where you save
your work, like recording on
a video tape.

10. **DOCUMENT**: Anything you
create in Microsoft Word is
called a document.

11. **FILE**: a piece of
computer information such
as a document or part of a

computer program.

12. **FOLDER**: Just like a file folder in a filing cabinet, a file is where documents (letters, spreadsheets, etc.) are kept.

13. **FONT**: The way letters and words look.

14. **FORMAT:** Changing the way that text looks on the page.

THIS _is_ formatted.

This is not formatted.

15. **HARDWARE**: All the parts of the computer that you can touch: the monitor, CPU, printer, mouse, and keyboard.

16. **HARD DRIVE:** the place inside your computer where programs and files are stored.

17. HIGHLIGHT/SELECTING:

Click and drag across a word or sentence to highlight it. When it is highlighted you can make changes to it.

18. **ICON**: Symbols or pictures that you can click on to perform an action. Each program has its own icon.

19. **ITALICS**: A font style that slants words to the right. 20. **KEYBOARD:** Like a typewriter, it's where you type and enter numbers. It is one way to tell the computer what you want it to do.

21. **MENU BAR**: The words at the top of the screen. Click on these words and you see menus of other things you can do.

22. **MENU**: A list of other

things you can do. You see
a menu when you click on
one of the words on the
Menu Bar.

23. MICROSOFT WORD: A
word-processing program
for typing letters, resumes,
school papers and more.

24. : **MONITOR:** Your
computer's screen

25. MOUSE: The tool you
can use tell the computer
what to do. For example
you can open programs and
files by clicking or double
clicking.

26. **OPEN:** A command on
the File Menu that brings
files onto the screen so that
you can see them.

27. POINT: The size of text.
12 point 16 point 24 point

28. PROGRAMS: Another

word for software or
applications.

29. **SCREEN SAVER:** A
design on the screen that
turns on if you don't use
your computer for a few
minutes.

30. SCROLL BARS: The bars
on the sides of the screen
that allow you to move up
or down the page.

31. SPREADSHEET:
Organizes information into
rows and columns and
often uses math and
numbers.

32. TOOL BARS: The bars
across the top of the screen
that have info for your page.

Windows Specific Computer Terms

Hardware

- The physical parts of a computer -

CPU

Central processing unit; the brain of the computer; controls the other elements
of the computer

Disk Drive

A peripheral device that reads and/or writes information on a disk

Hard Drive

A device (usually within the computer case) that reads and writes information,
including the operating system, program files, and data files

Keyboard

A peripheral used to input data by pressing keys
Modem

A peripheral device used to connect one computer to another over a phone line

Monitor

A device used to display information visually

Mouse

A peripheral device used to point to items on a monitor

NIC

Network interface card; a board inserted in a computer that provides a physical
connection to a network

Printer

A peripheral device that converts output from a computer into a printed image

Software

- Instructions executed by a computer -

Applications

Complete, self-contained programs that perform a specific function (ie. spreadsheets, databases)

Bit

A computer's most basic unit of information

Boot

The process of loading or initializing an operating system on a computer; usually occurs as soon as a computer is turned on

Browser

A program used to view World Wide Web pages, such as Netscape Navigator or
Internet Explorer

Bug

A part of a program that usually causes the computer to malfunction; often remedied in patches or updates to the program

Byte

Small unit of data storage; 8 bits; usually holds one character

Click

Occurs when a user presses a button on a mouse which in turn, generates a command to the computer

Database

A large structured set of data; a file that contains numerous records that contain numerous fields

Diskette

A small flexible disk used for storing computer data

Double Click

Occurs when a user presses a button on the mouse twice in quick succession; this
generates a command to the computer

Download

Transferring data from another computer to your computer

Drag

Occurs when a user points the mouse at an icon or folder, presses the button and
without releasing the button, moves the icon or folder to another place on the
computer where the button is released

Driver

Software program that controls a piece of hardware or a peripheral

FAQ

Frequently asked question; documents that answer questions common to a particular website or program

File

Namable unit of data storage; an element of data storage; a single sequence of
bytes

Folder

A graphical representation used to organize a collection of computer files; as in the concept of a filing cabinet (computer's hard drive) with files (folders)

Freeware

Software provided at no cost to the user

Gigabyte

1,073,741,824 bytes or 1,024 megabytes; generally abbreviated GB

GUI

Graphical user interface; uses pictures and words to represent ideas, choices, functions, etc.

Icon

A small picture used to represent a file or program in a GUI interface

Internet

A network of computer networks encompassing the World Wide Web, FTP, telnet, and
many other protocols

IP number

Internet protocol; a computer's unique address or number on the Internet

Kilobyte

1,024 bytes; usually abbreviated KB

Megabyte

1,048,576 bytes or 1,024 kilobytes; enough storage to approximately equal a 600
page paperback book; generally abbreviated Mb

Memory

Any device that holds computer data

Menu

A list of operations available to the user of a program

Network

A collection of computers that are connected

Peripheral

Any of a number of hardware devices connected to a CPU

RAM

Random access memory; the type of storage that changes; when the computer is
turned off, the RAM memory is erased

ROM

Read-only memory; the type of storage that is not changed even when the computer
is turned off

Scroll Bar

Allows the user to control which portion of the document is visible in the
window; available either horizontally or vertically or both

Shareware

Software provided at a minimal cost to users who are on their honor to send in
payment to the programmer

Spreadsheet

A program arranged in rows and columns that manipulates numbers

Tool Bar

A graphical representation of program activities; a row of icons used to perform
tasks in a program

URL

Uniform resource locator; the address of a site on the World Wide Web; a standard way of locating objects on the Internet

Virus

A deliberately harmful computer program designed to create annoying glitches or destroy data

Window

A screen in a software program that permits the user to view several programs at one time

Word Processor

A program that allows the user to create primarily text documents.

Glossary of Computer and New Internet Terms

1 Address Box

A narrow, rectangular box in the browser window where you can type in a web address. Typing in the web address in the address box and hitting Enter on the keyboard will take you to a website.

Address Box Web Address (URL)

2Back Arrow

This arrow, often green, is found at the top of most browsers. When you click on the back arrow, it takes you back – in order – through all of the web pages you've seen. (Sometimes called the back button.)

3 Browse

To explore a website or a number of websites by scanning and reading information.

4 Browser

Software, such as Microsoft Internet Explorer, used to find information on the Web. The most visible part of a browser sits at the top of the computer screen, above the web page.

5 Button

Small box that looks like it's being depressed when you select it. Buttons can turn on (and turn off) many types of functions on the Internet.

6 Clicking

Pressing and releasing a button on a mouse to select or activate the area on the screen where the cursor is pointing. Usually, you click on the left side of the mouse (called a left click). For more advanced functions, you click on the right side of the mouse (called a right click).

7 Computer or CPU(central processing unit)

The main part, or "brains" of a compute. The CPU interprets and carries out program instructions.

8 Cursor

A small image on the screen indicating where you are pointing; the mouse controls the movements of the cursor. The cursor can appear in different forms, including:

> An arrow, which indicates where you are positioned on the screen.

> An I-beam, often blinking, which marks a place on the screen where you can enter or select text.

> A pointing hand, which indicates that you are hovering over a link. (See **Link**.)

An hourglass, which indicates that the computer is doing a task. You must wait until it disappears before you can proceed.

9 Desktop

The information that appears on the computer soon after the computer is turned on. The desktop contains a number of icons, or images, that you can click on to start programs. (See **icon**.)

10 Dialog Box

A special box that appears when the computer needs additional information in order to carry out a task. This dialog box appears in a quiz on the NIHSeniorHealth website whenever you try to advance to the next quiz question without answering the current one. (You must click on "ok" to have a dialog box disappear.)

11 Icon

A list of items from which you can make selections.

A. When you first see a box containing a drop down list, the box will be empty or may display only a single item.

B. To see a list of choices, left click on the arrow in the box and hold. The list of choices will display above or below the box.

C. Keeping your left index finger pressed on the mouse, move the cursor to the desired choice (In this case, a quantity of 3 booklets).

D. Release your left index finger from the mouse, and your selection will appear in the box. The full list of choices will disappear.

12 FAQs

Stands for **F**requently **A**sked **Q**uestions. These are commonly asked questions and answers that appear on many websites.

A B C D

The Microsoft Management Console (MMC).

The Microsoft Management Console MMC is built into every Windows. To access the mmc just type into the computer RUN or START window the word " mmc" to display the MMC Console Root Window.

The mmc utility allows the user to create a special troubleshooting small Utility called a "SNAPIN "from a series of pre-built Snapins already integrated into the software console root.

Step-by-Step Guide to the Microsoft Management Console

Introduction

MMC unifies and simplifies day-to-day system management tasks. It hosts tools and displays them as consoles. These tools, consisting of one or more applications, are built with modules called snap-ins. The snap-ins also can include additional extension snap-ins. MMC is a core part of Microsoft's management strategy and is included in Microsoft Windows® 2000 operating systems. In addition, Microsoft development groups will use MMC for future management applications.

Microsoft Management Console enables system administrators to create special tools to delegate specific administrative tasks to users or groups. Microsoft provides standard tools with the operating system that perform everyday administrative tasks that users need to accomplish. These are part of the **All Users** profile of the computer and located in the **Administrative Tools** group on the **Startup** menu. Saved as MMC console (.msc) files, these custom tools can be sent by e-mail, shared in a network folder, or posted on the Web. They can also be assigned to users, groups, or computers with system policy settings. A tool can be scaled up and down, integrated seamlessly into the operating system, repackaged, and customized.

Using MMC, system administrators can create unique consoles for workers who report to them or for workgroup managers. They can assign a tool with a system policy, deliver the file by e-mail, or post the file to a shared location on the network. When a workgroup manager opens the .msc file, access will be restricted to those tools provided by the system administrator.

Building your own tools with the standard user interface in MMC is a straightforward process. Start with an existing console and modify or add components to fulfill your needs. Or create an entirely new console. The following example shows how to create a new console and arrange its administrative components into separate windows.

Prerequisites and Requirements

There are no prerequisites: you don't need to complete any other step-by-step guide before starting this guide. You need one computer running either Windows 2000 Professional or Windows 2000 Server. For the most current information about hardware requirements and compatibility for servers, clients, and peripherals, see the Check Hardware and Software Compatibility page on the Windows 2000 website.

Creating Consoles

The most common way for administrators to use MMC is to simply start a predefined console file from the Start menu. However, to get an idea of the flexibility of MMC, it is useful to create a console file from scratch. It is also useful to create a console file from scratch when using the new task delegation features in this version of MMC.

Creating a New Console File

On the Start Menu, click **Run**, type **MMC**, and then click **OK**. Microsoft Management Console opens with an empty console (or administrative tool) as shown in Figure 1 below. The empty console has no management functionality until you add some snap-ins. The MMC menu commands on the menu bar at the top of the Microsoft Management Console window apply to the entire console.

Figure 1: Beginning Console Window

Click Console (under Console1). On the Console Menu, click **Add/Remove Snap-in**. The Add/Remove Snap-in dialog box opens. This lets you enable extensions and configure which snap-ins are in the console file. You can specify where the snap-ins should be inserted in the **Snap-in's "added to** drop-down box." Accept the default, **Console Root**, for this exercise.

Click **Add**. This displays the Add Standalone Snap-in dialog box that lists the snap-ins that are installed on your computer.

From the list of snap-ins, double-click **Computer Management** to open the **Computer Management** wizard.

Click **Local computer** and select the check box for "**Allow the selected computer to be changed when launching from the command line**."

Click **Finish**. This returns you to the **Add/Remove Snap-ins** dialog box. Click **Close**.

Click the **Extensions** tab as shown in Figure 2 below. By selecting the check box **Add all extensions**, all locally-installed extensions on the computer are used. If this check box is not selected, then any extension snap-in that is selected is explicitly loaded when the console file is opened on a different computer.

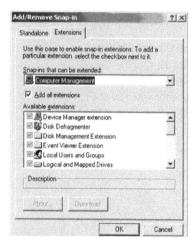

Figure 2: Select All Extensions

Click **OK** to close the Add/Remove Snap-in dialog box. The Console Root window now has a snap-in, **Computer Management**, rooted at the Console Root folder.

Customizing the Display of Snap-ins in the Console: New Windows

After you add the snap-ins, you can add windows to provide a different administrative views in the console.

To add windows

1. In the left pane of the tree view in Figure 3 below, click the **+** next to **Computer Management**. Click **System Tools**.

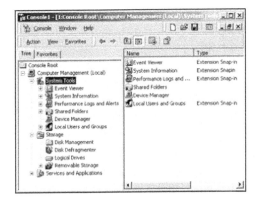

Figure 3: Console1: System Tools

2. Right-click the **Event Viewer** folder that opens, and then click **New window** from here. As shown in Figure 4 below, this opens a new Event Viewer window rooted at the Event Viewer extension to computer management.

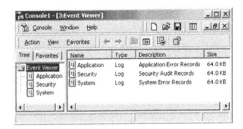

Figure 4: Event Viewer

3. Click **Window** and click **Console Root**.

4. In the Console Root window, click **Services and Applications**, right-click **Services** in the left pane, and then click **New Window**. As shown in Figure 5 below, this opens a new Services window rooted at the Event Viewer extension to Computer Management. In the new window, click the **Show/Hide Console Tree** toolbar button to hide the console tree, as shown in the red circle in Figure 5 below.

Figure 5: Show/Hide Button

5. Close the original window with Console Root showing in it.

6. On the Window menu, select **Tile Horizontally**. The console file should appear and include the information shown in Figure 4 and Figure 5 above.

7. You can now save your new MMC console. Click the **Save as** icon on the Console window, and give your console a name. Your console is now saved as a .msc file, and you can provide it to anyone who needs to configure a computer with these tools.

Note: Each of the two smaller windows has a toolbar with buttons and drop-down menus. The toolbar buttons and drop-down menus on these each of these two windows apply only to the contents of the window. You can see that a window's toolbar buttons and menus change depending on the snap-in selected in the left pane of the window. If you select the View menu, you can see a list of available toolbars.

Tip: The windows fit better if your monitor display is set to a higher resolution and small font.

Creating Console Taskpads

If you are creating a console file for another user, it's useful to provide a very simplified view with only a few tasks available. Console taskpads help you to do this.

To create a console taskpad

6. From the Window menu, select **New Window**. Close the other two

windows (you will save a new console file at the end of this procedure). Maximize the remaining window.

7. In the left pane, click the + next to the **Computer Management** folder, then click the + next to the **System Tools** folder. Click **System**, click the **Event Viewer** folder, right-click **System**, and select **New Taskpad** View.

8. Go through the wizard accepting all the default settings. Verify the checkbox on the last page is checked so that the Task Creation wizard can start automatically.

9. Choose the defaults in the Task Creation wizard until you come to the page shown below in Figure 6, then choose a list view task and select **Properties**:

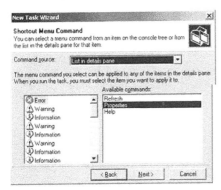

Figure 6: New Task Wizard

10. Click **Next** and accept the defaults for the rest of the screens. By selecting an Event and clicking **Properties**, you can see the property page for that Event.

After you click **Finish** on the last screen, your console should look like Figure 7 below:

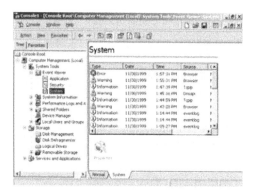

Figure 7: New Console Showing System Event Log

11. Click the **Show/Hide console tree** toolbar button.

12. From the view menu, click **Customize** and click each of the options except the Description bar to hide each type of toolbar.

The next section discusses how to lock the console file down so that the user sees only a limited view. For right now your console file should look like Figure 8 below.

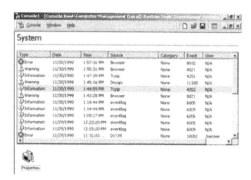

Figure 8: Customized View

Setting Console File Options

If you are creating a console file for another user, it is useful to prevent that user from further customizing the console file. The Options dialog box allows you to do this.

To set console file options

1. From the **Console** menu, select **Options**.
2. Change the Console Mode by selecting **User Modelimited access, single   window** from the drop-down dialog box. This will prevent a user from adding new snap-ins to the console file or rearranging the windows.
3. You can change the name from Console1. Click **OK** to continue.
4. **Save** the console file. The changes will not take effect until the console file is opened again.

This is just one example of how the Microsoft Management Console lets you group information and functionality that previously would have required opening a Control Panel option plus two separate administrative tools. The modular architecture of MMC makes it easy for users to create snap-in applications that leverage the platform while easing administrative load.

This is not the End.

www.ingramcontent.com/pod-product-compliance
Lightning Source LLC
Chambersburg PA
CBHW070836070326
40690CB00009B/1577